# INTRODUCTION

The National Curriculum in Mathematics has been divided into five areas which are contained in the tests in this book. The tests contain much of the work to be covered by the end of Key Stage 2.

The material can be used to highlight the areas with which the child is unfamiliar or which need explanation and further practice.

There is no time limit

Rough work may be done in the book but preferably blank paper for this purpose should be provided. A ruler and protractor will be needed for some of the questions.

Many of the mathematical terms used in the units are explained in the glossary.

# GLOSSARY

**Angles**

An angle is the amount of turn from one line to another. Angles are measured in degrees. A *right angle* measures 90° and an *acute angle* is less than 90°. An *obtuse angle* is more than 90° but less than 180°. A *reflex angle* is more than 180° but less than 360°.

**Area**

The area of a surface is the amount of space it occupies. The area of a rectangle is found by multiplying the length by the breadth. The area of a triangle is half the length of the base times the perpendicular height.

**Average** (See mean)

**Co-ordinates**

A pair of numbers used to locate a point on a grid.

**Cube**

A cuboid with square faces and all its edges the same length.

**Cubed Numbers**

A number is cubed when it is multiplied by itself twice.
e.g. 5 cubed is 5 x 5 x 5, written as $5^3$.
$5^3 = 125$

**Cuboid**

A solid with all six faces rectangular.

**Faces**

The flat sides of a solid shape.

**Factors**

Any number which can be divided exactly into another number is a factor of that number.
eg. the factors of 12 are:- 1, 2, 3, 4, 6 and 12.
*Common factors* are the factors which are common or shared by various numbers.
eg. The factors of 12: - <u>1</u>, 2, <u>3</u>, 4, 6, 12.
   The factors of 9 are:- <u>1</u>, <u>3</u>, 9.
   The common factors of 9 and 12 are 1 and 3.
   The *highest common factor* of 9 and 12 is 3.

**Gram (g)**

The standard unit used in weighing.
1000 g = 1 kg (Kilogram)
(See metric conversions)

**Hexagon**

A six sided figure. A regular hexagon has six equal sides and six equal angles.

**Horizontal**

A line is horizontal if it is parallel to the horizon.

**Index Form**

When a number is written as the power of another number it is said to be in index form.
$5^2$ is in the index form of 25
$8^2$ is the index form of 64 and so is $4^3$
(see square and cubed numbers)

**Kite**

A four sided figure with two pairs of equal sides which are not opposite to each other.

**Litre (1)**

The standard unit used in measuring liquids.
1 litre = 1000 ml (millilitres)
(See metric conversions)

**Mean**

Mean is another name for average. To find the mean of six numbers add the numbers together and divide the result by six.

**Median**

When a set of numbers is arranged in order of size the middle number in the new order is known as the median.

**Metre (m)**

The standard unit used in measuring length.
1 metre = 100 cm (centimetres)
1 cm = 10mm (millimetres)
1 kilometre = 1000 metres
(See metric conversions)

**Metric Conversions**

Approximate imperial measures.

1 litre = 1.75 pints
4.5 litres = 1 gallon
1 kilogram = 2.2 pounds
1 metre = 3.3 feet
1 kilometre = 0.62 miles
8 kilometres = 5 miles

**Multiples**

The multiples of a number are obtained by multiplying the number by the counting number (1, 2, 3, 4, 5 etc).
eg. The multiples of 3 are 3, 6, 9, 12, 15, 18 etc.
*Common multiples* are the multiples which are common to or shared by various numbers.
eg. Multiples of 3:- 3, 6, 9, 12, 15, 18, 21, 24, 17 etc
   Multiples of 4:- 4, 8, 12, 16, 20, 24, 28 etc
   Some of the common multiples of 3 and 4 are
   12 and 24.

**Net**

A net is formed when the sides of a solid are folded out and laid flat.

**Oblique**

Oblique lines are slanting lines. Lines which are neither vertical nor horizontal are oblique.

**Parallel**

Lines are parallel if all their points are always the same distance apart.

**Parallelogram**

A four sided figure formed by two pairs of parallel lines.

**Pentagon**

A five sided figure. A regular pentagon has five equal sides and five equal angles.

**Perimeter**

The distance around a shape.
A rectangle with sides of 7cm and 3cm has a perimeter of 20cm (7 + 7 + 3 + 3).

**Perpendicular**

When two lines cross at right angles they are said to be perpendicular.

**Prime Numbers**

A prime number is a number that can only be divided by itself and the number 1 and therefore has only two factors. (see Factors)
eg. The factors of 11 are 1 and 11.
   The factors of 19 are 1 and 19.
   The prime numbers are 2, 3, 5, 7, 11, 13, 17, 19, 23, etc.

**Prism**

A solid shape with flat sides. A prism has the same shape along its length.

**Probability**

The likelihood or not of an event occurring is its probability.
The probability of a new baby being a girl is $1/2$.
The probability of throwing a four on a die is $1/6$.
The probability of throwing an even number on a die is $1/2$.

**Pyramid**

A solid shape with flat sides. It is made up of a base and triangular sides which meet at a point called the apex.

**Rectangle**

A four sided figure with opposite sides equal and parallel and four right angles.

Glossary continued on inside back cover.

# HANDLING DATA

SCORE:    TEST ONE _____

TEST TWO _____

This tally chart shows the number of people who entered a shopping centre during a 5 minute period one day. Complete the table to show the number of women, boys and girls.

|  | Number of People | Total |
|---|---|---|
| Men | ⊥⊥⊥⊥ ⊥⊥⊥⊥ I | 11 |
| **1** Women | ⊥⊥⊥⊥ ⊥⊥⊥⊥ ⊥⊥⊥⊥ ⊥⊥⊥⊥<br>⊥⊥⊥⊥ ⊥⊥⊥⊥ ⊥⊥⊥⊥ III |  |
| **2** Boys | ⊥⊥⊥⊥ II |  |
| **3** Girls | ⊥⊥⊥⊥ ⊥⊥⊥⊥ ⊥⊥⊥⊥ IIII |  |

**4** How many children went to the centre?

Ans _____ children

**5** How many adults?

Ans _____ adults

**6** How many more women than men?

Ans _____ women

This graph shows the maximum and minimum temperatures, measured in degrees celsius, for 4 towns A,B,C and D for the same day.

TEMPERATURE vs TOWNS (A, B, C, D)

**7** Which town had the lowest temperature that day?

Ans _____

**8** Which town had the highest temperature?

Ans _____

**9** Which town had the biggest difference in temperature?

Ans _____

**10** Which town had the smallest difference in temperature?

Ans _____

**11** How many towns were hotter than 17°C?

Ans _____

**12** How many towns were colder than 8°C?

Ans _____

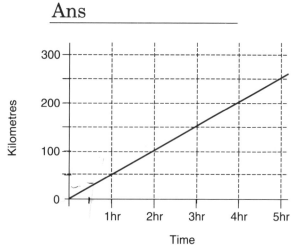

The graph above shows a car travelling at a steady speed. Read from the graph how many km the car travels in -

**13** 30 min _____ km  **14** 2 hr _____ km

**15** $3\frac{1}{2}$ hr _____ km  **16** $4\frac{1}{2}$ hr _____ km

How long will it take the car to travel?

**17** 75 km _____ hr _____ min

**18** 100 km _____ hr _____ min

**19** 125 km _____ hr _____ min

**20** 250 km _____ hr _____ min

The table shows the amount of pocket money given to five children - A,B,C,D and E.

| Child | A | B | C | D | E |
|-------|------|------|------|------|------|
| Money | £1.50 | £4.00 | £2.50 | £4.50 | £2.50 |

Complete the bar chart to show how much each child received.

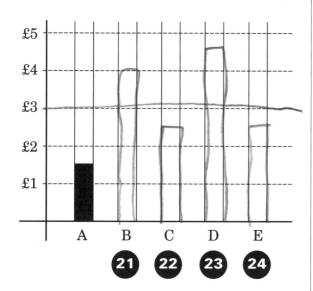

**25** Draw a line across the graph to show the average.

**26** What was the average amount received?

Ans £ _____

**27** How many children received more than the average amount?

Ans _____

The timetable shows the times of buses from Pipton to Stenup and also of buses travelling in the opposite direction.

| OUTWARD | | | RETURN | |
|---------|-------|---------|-------|-------|
| 07.15 | 15.30 | Pipton | 12.55 | 20.40 |
| 07.50 | 16.05 | Batley | 12.20 | 20.05 |
| 08.15 | 16.30 | Carslow | 11.55 | 19.40 |
| 08.55 | 17.10 | Radford | 11.15 | 19.00 |
| 09.40 | 17.55 | Stenup | 10.30 | 18.15 |

**28** At what time does the 15.30 bus from Pipton arrive in Radford? _____

**29** When does the 10.30 bus from Stenup arrive at Carslow? _____

**30** How long does it take to travel from Pipton to Stenup? _____hr _____min

**31** How long does it take to go from Radford to Batley? _____hr _____min

**32** Four buses stop at Carslow each day. When could I board the second bus there? _____

**33** If the 11.15 from Radford is running 15 minutes late, when will I arrive at Batley? _____

**34** A man living in Stenup has an appointment in Batley at 13·15. Which bus, from Stenup, must he take to arrive on time for his appointment?

Ans _____

**35** If I travel from Batley to Stenup on the first bus and return on the last bus, at what time will I arrive back at Batley? _____

The pie chart shows the colours of 120 cars parked in a car park. Show the same information on the bar chart below.

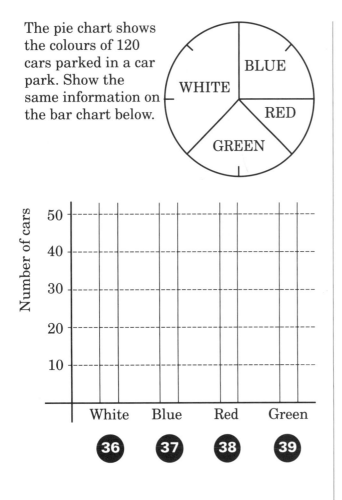

State the number of cars of each colour.

**40** White cars _____

**41** Blue cars_____

**42** Red cars _____

**43** Green cars _____

The graph shows the daily takings of two shops, A and B, over a ten day period.

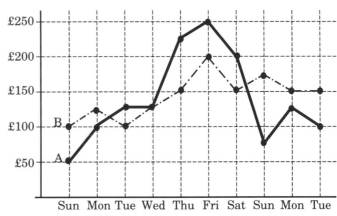

**44** How much was lifted by shop A on the first Tuesday?  £ _____

**45** How much was lifted by shop B on the Thursday?  £ _____

**46** On which day did both shops lift the same amount?

Ans _____

**47** What was the total takings for shop B on the two Sundays?  £ _____

**48** What was the total takings for shop A on the two Mondays?  £ _____

**49** On which day of the week were both shops the busiest?

Ans _____

**50** What is the difference between shop A's lowest and highest takings?

Ans £ _____

This table shows the number of tyres sold by 7 garages during July. The garages are called A, B, C, D, E, F and G.

| Garage | A | B | C | D | E | F | G |
|---|---|---|---|---|---|---|---|
| No of Tyres sold in July | 1000 | 4250 | 750 | 2750 | 1750 | 1250 | 3500 |

Put this information on the block graph below. Garage A has been completed for you.

TYRES SOLD IN JULY

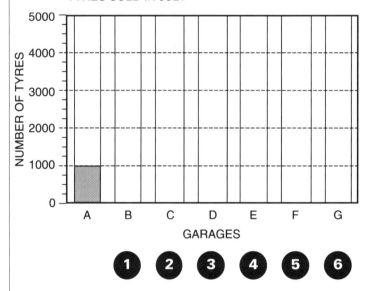

Complete this tally chart of the number of televisions in different houses. Fill in the spaces.

| Number of Televisions | Number of Houses | Total number of Houses |
|---|---|---|
| 1 | ЖHТ ЖHТ ЖHТ ЖHТ ЖHТ ΙΙ | 27 |
| 2 | | 17 |
| 3 | ЖHТ | |
| 4 | | 9 |
| 5 | ЖHТ ΙΙ | |
| 6 or more | ΙΙ | |

**12** Calculate the mean (average) of

8    3    4    9    16    12    11

Ans _____

**13** What is the median of the following numbers?

15  12  7  8  3  50  11

Ans _____

Complete this table of the earnings of part-time waiters in a hotel.

| Waiter | Earnings | Hours worked | Average pay per hour |
|--------|----------|--------------|----------------------|
| A | £32 | 8 | £4 |
| B | £24.50 | 7 | £_____ |
| C | £24 | _____ | £3 |
| D | £_____ | 11 | £2.50 |

**14** (row B)
**15** (row C)
**16** (row D)

Look at this bar-line graph and answer the following questions.

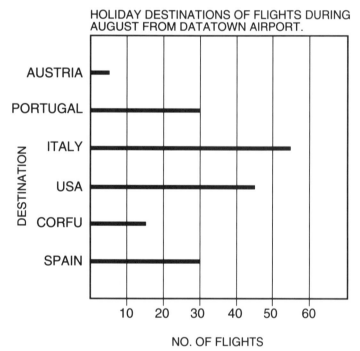

HOLIDAY DESTINATIONS OF FLIGHTS DURING AUGUST FROM DATATOWN AIRPORT.

NO. OF FLIGHTS

**17** Which was the most popular destination?

Ans _____

**18** Which was the least popular destination?

Ans _____

**19** Which two destinations had the same number of flights?

_____ AND _____

**20** How many flights went to Corfu?

Ans _____

**21** How many more flights went to the U.S.A. than to Spain?

Ans _____

Look at this line graph. It represents a trip into the countryside by a cyclist. The distance from home is marked against time. Answer the questions that follow the graph.

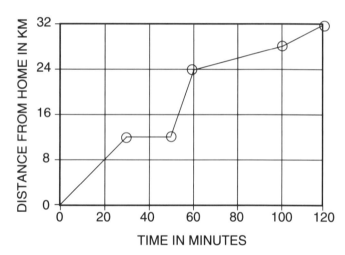

TIME IN MINUTES

**22** How far has the cyclist gone after 10 mins?

Ans _____ km

**23** How far does he travel between 30 min and 50 min? Circle one answer.

6km    1km    3km    0km    4km

**24** How long after leaving home does he begin to travel at his fastest speed?

Ans _____ min

HANDLING DATA TEST TWO PAGE 2

**25** How long does it take him to travel 28 km?

Ans _____ min

**26** What is his average speed is km/h for the whole journey?

Ans _____ km/h

**27** What is the probability of throwing a six on a true, fair die (single dice) marked from 1-6?

Ans _____

**28** What is the probability of throwing an odd number on the same die?

Ans _____

**29** What is the probability of obtaining a "tail" when a fair coin is tossed?

Ans _____

This pie chart shows the types of dogs entered in a dog show. There were 80 dogs altogether.

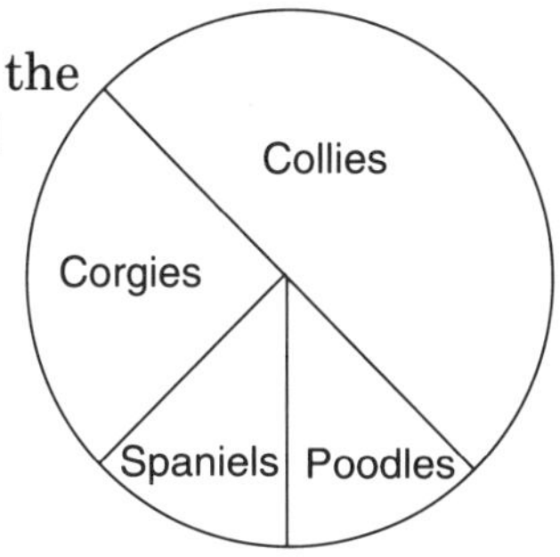

Collies

Corgies

Spaniels Poodles

**30** How many corgies were in the dog show?

Ans _____ corgies

**31** What fraction of the dogs were spaniels?

Ans _____

**32** How many of the dogs were either collies or poodles?

Ans _____

Look at this Venn diagram. It shows the possessions of 8 children called A, B, C, D, E, F, G and H .

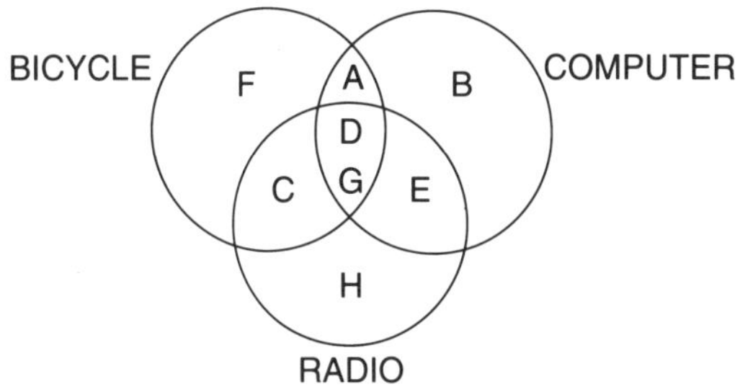

BICYCLE      F   A   B   COMPUTER
                 D
             C  G  E
                 H
              RADIO

**33** Who has a computer and radio but no bicycle?

Ans _____

**34** Who has a bicycle and a radio but doesn't have a computer?

Ans _____

**35** What 2 things does A have?

_____ AND _____

**36** Who has a bicycle and a computer but doesn't own a radio?

Ans _____

**37** Which 2 people have a bicycle, computer and radio?

_____ AND _____

The information in this table shows some things that 6 cars A, B, C, D, E and F may or may not have. Place the information into the Venn diagram. The information about car "A" has been entered for you.

| Name of Car | Hatch back | Metallic Paint | Radio |
|---|---|---|---|
| A | ✔ | ✗ | ✔ |
| B | ✔ | ✔ | ✔ |
| C | ✗ | ✔ | ✔ |
| D | ✗ | ✗ | ✔ |
| E | ✔ | ✔ | ✗ |
| F | ✗ | ✔ | ✗ |

(38) B
(39) C
(40) D
(41) E
(42) F

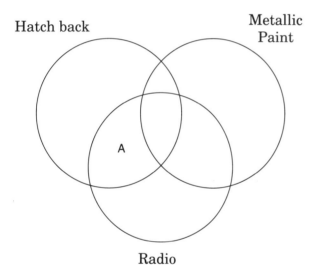

Hatch back

Metallic Paint

Radio

Black (B), green (G), white (W) and yellow (Y) paint are mixed two colours at a time. All the combinations except 3 have been given. Write the missing combinations below.

B&W   G&W   W&Y

(43) _____ AND _____

(44) _____ AND _____

(45) _____ AND _____

This table shows the percentage of different books in a library.

| Book | Percentage |
|---|---|
| Sport | 25% |
| History | $12\frac{1}{2}\%$ |
| Science | 50% |
| Art | $6\frac{1}{4}\%$ |
| Music | $6\frac{1}{4}\%$ |

(46) Sport
(47) History
(48) Science
(49) Art
(50) Music

Divide this circle into sectors and label it to represent the information in the table.

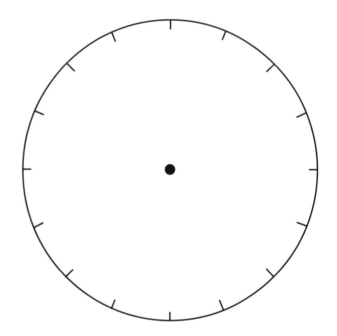

# MEASURES

SCORE:   TEST ONE_____

TEST TWO_____

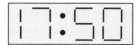

This digital clock display is 20 minutes slow. What is the correct time? Show your answer in two ways.

**1** [ : ]

Digital Clock

**2**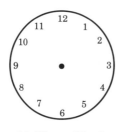

12 Hour Clock

Bus departure times are shown below. Write each time as a 24 hour clock time.

| | 12 Hour Clock | 24 Hour Clock |
|---|---|---|
| **3** | 7·40am | _____ |
| **4** | 11·20am | _____ |
| **5** | 3·30pm | _____ |
| **6** | 7·50pm | _____ |
| **7** | 10·10pm | _____ |

**8** How many minutes in $1\frac{3}{4}$ hours?

Ans _____ min

**9** How many hours in $2\frac{1}{2}$ days?

Ans _____ hours

**10** How long does it take to boil an egg? Circle one answer.

1 hour    4min    48min    15sec    120min

**11** Approximately how long should it take to walk 1 kilometre? Circle one answer.

3 min    5 min    12 min    50 min    $1\frac{1}{4}$ hours

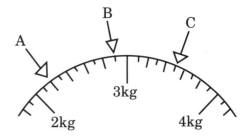

The diagram shows part of the scale on a weighing machine. What weight is shown at points A, B and C?

**12** A _____ kg _____ g

**13** B _____ kg _____ g

**14** C _____ kg _____ g

**15** What is the difference in grams from point A to point C?

Ans _____ g

Complete the following.

**16** 650g + [ ] g = 1kg

**17** 2kg - 1kg 600g = [ ] g

**18** 1100g + [ ] g = 1·5kg

In the following questions circle the most sensible weight.

**19** A new born baby would weigh -

3kg    30g    50kg    400g    1000g

**20** An orange would weigh -

1kg    2kg    10g    200g    800g

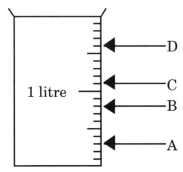

1 litre

This container holds 2 litres of water. How much water would be in the container at each level?

**21** Level A _____ ml

**22** Level B _____ ml

**23** Level C _____ ml

**24** Level D _____ ml

**25** If the container had water up to level C how much more water would be needed to fill it?

Ans _____ ml

How many millilitres in -

**26** $\frac{1}{4}$ litre _____ ml

**27** 2·3 litres _____ ml

**28** 4 litres 250ml _____ ml

Chose one amount to complete each statement. Circle your answer.

**29** An egg cup would hold -

1 litre    5ml    50ml    100ml    200ml

**30** The petrol tank of a motorbike would hold -

12 litres    110 litres    1500ml    35000ml

**31** 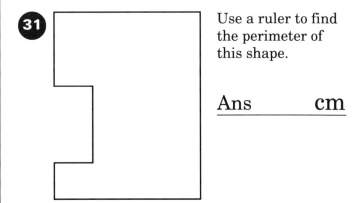 Use a ruler to find the perimeter of this shape.

Ans _____ cm

**32** Which has the biggest perimeter? Tick one box.

A square with an area of 81cm² ☐

A rectangle with sides of 10cm and 4cm ☐

Calculate the area of these shapes. (The shapes are not drawn to scale)

**33** 6cm

5cm    Ans _____ cm²

**34**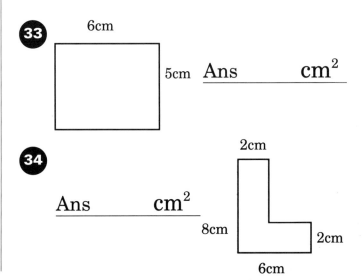

Ans _____ cm²

**35** The area of a room is 54m$^2$. If the room is 9m long, how wide is it?

Ans _____ m

**36** How many cuboids make up this solid shape?

Ans _____ cuboids

6cm

20cm

8cm

**37** What is the volume of this block of wood?

Ans _____ cm$^3$

**38** The volume of a shoe box is 2400cm$^3$. If the box is 20cm long and 12cm wide what height is it?

Ans _____ cm

Each line below is drawn to a different scale. Measure each line to the nearest cm and use the scale to find the true length each time.

**39** _____
Scale 1cm to 10cm

True Length (_____) cm

**40** _____
Scale 1cm to 30cm

True Length (_____) cm

**41** _____
Scale 1cm to 2m

True Length (_____) m

**42** _____
Scale 1cm to 5km

True Length (_____) km

**43** _____
Scale 1cm to 20km

True Length (_____) km

Living Room | Hall

Dining Room | Kitchen

This is the ground floor plan of a house. The plan is drawn to a scale of 1cm to 2 metres. Measure the rooms to the nearest cm and work out the true length and breadth of -

**44** The Hall _____ m and _____ m

**45** The Living Room _____ m and _____ m

**46** The Kitchen _____ m and _____ m

Measure these angles.

**47**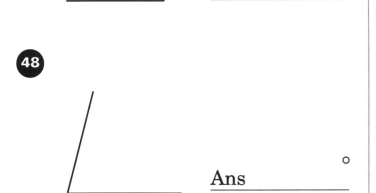

Ans _____ °

**48**

Ans _____ °

Circle one answer in each of the following.

**49** The petrol tank of a car holds 10 **gallons.** Approximately how many litres is **this?**

10          25          45          60          **100**

**50** Potatoes are sold in 3kg bags. **What is the** approximate weight in pounds?

2          6·5          10          12·5          **15**

---

## TEST TWO

---

**1** 1m 30cm = (_____) cm

**2** 2156 millitres = (_____) litres

**3** 3 hours 12 min = (_____) min

**4** A $\frac{3}{4}$ turn = (_____) degrees

**5** A square has sides each measuring 8·5 cm. What is the perimeter of the square?

Ans _____ cm

**6** A regular hexagon has sides each measuring 4·1 cm. What is the perimeter of the hexagon?

Ans _____ cm

**7** What is the name given to the distance around the outside of a circle?

Ans _____

**8** 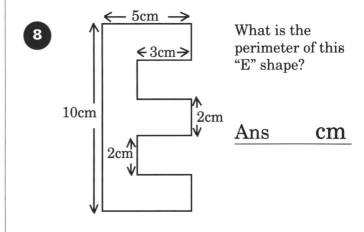 What is the perimeter of this "E" shape?

Ans _____ cm

**9** What is the area of a rectangular swimming pool which has a long side of 7m and a short side of 4m?

Ans _____ m$^2$

**10**

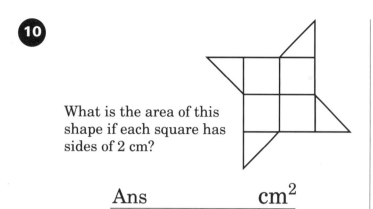

What is the area of this shape if each square has sides of 2 cm?

Ans _____ cm$^2$

**11** What is the volume of a chocolate box measuring 3cm x 15cm x 30cm?

Ans _____ cm$^3$

**12**

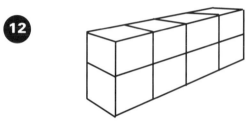

What is the volume of this shape if one cuboid has a volume of 12 cubic centimetres?

Ans _____ cm$^3$

**13** What is the approximate height of the front door of your home? Circle one answer.

2cm          10m          5m          2m          15cm

**14** Approximately how long would it take an olympic runner to run 100 metres? Circle one answer.

10 minutes          1 hour          1 day

10 seconds          1 week

**15** Approximately what would be the temperature (°C) on a very cold winter's day? Circle one answer.

100°          70°          0°          25°          50°

**16** Approximately how much lemonade is in a normal sized can? Circle one answer.

2 litres          $\frac{1}{2}$ litre          5 millitres

330 millitres          5 litres

**17**

This diagram shows the time on a 24 hour clock. What is this time on a 12 hour clock? Use am or pm.

Ans _____

**18** Write twenty five to nine in the evening as you would see it on a 24 hour clock.

Ans _____

**19**

This twenty four hour clock shows what time? Circle one answer.

8.45am          9.15pm          6.15pm

9.15am          4.15pm

**20** On the blank 24 hour clock face show the time $2\frac{1}{2}$ hours after this time.

**21** On a map a scale of 1cm to 5km is used. A road measures 4cm on the map. What is the length of the road in real life?

Ans _____ km

**22** On a map a scale of 1cm to 700 metres is used. If a river is 2100 metres long in real life what length would it be on the map?

Ans _____ cm

**23** In a drawing an architect draws a building 5cm high. If he is using a scale of 1cm to 2 metres what height is the building in real life?

Ans _____ m

**24** A scale of 1 to 100 means that the model is what fraction of the original? Circle one answer.

$\frac{1}{10}$     $\frac{1}{1}$     $\frac{100}{1}$     $\frac{1}{1000}$     $\frac{1}{100}$

**25** A litre of water is approximately how many pints? Circle one answer.

5     $1\frac{3}{4}$     $\frac{1}{2}$     $2\frac{1}{3}$     10

**26** 8 kilometres is approximately how many miles? Circle one answer.

10     7     1     5     9

**27** 1 kilogram is approximately how many pounds in weight? Circle one answer.

10     6     9     4     2

**28** 3 feet is approximately how many metres? Circle one answer.

5 m     3 m     1 m     8 m     4 m

**29** How many millimetres in 5cm?

Ans _____ mm

**30** 1·65 metres is how many centimetres?

Ans _____ cm

**31** Write 1525 grams in kilograms using a decimal point.

Ans _____ kg

**32** How many millitres in 1.7 litres?

Ans _____ ml

**33** Using a protractor calculate this angle.

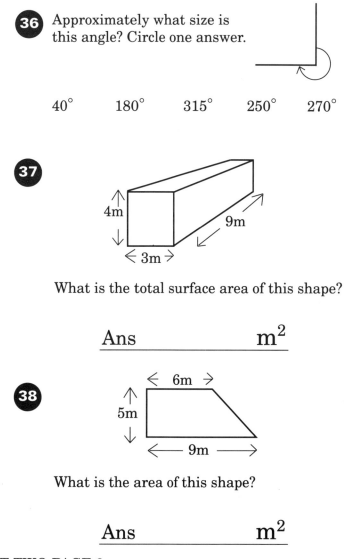

Ans _____

**34** How many right angles in one complete rotation?

Ans _____

**35** Circle any angle from this list which is an obtuse angle.

47°     74°     96°     227°     195°     315°

**36** Approximately what size is this angle? Circle one answer.

40°     180°     315°     250°     270°

**37**

What is the total surface area of this shape?

Ans _____ m$^2$

**38**

What is the area of this shape?

Ans _____ m$^2$

**39**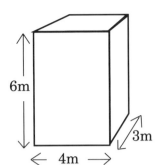

What is the volume of this shape?

Ans _____ m³

**40**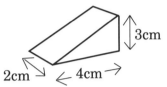

What is the volume of this shape?

Ans _____ cm³

**41** A train travels 15km in 15min. What is its speed in km/hour?

Ans _____ km/hour

**42** A plane flies 900km in 1½ hours. What is its speed in km/hour?

Ans _____ km/hour

**43** A conveyor belt travels at a rate of 2 metres every second. What is its speed in metres/hour?

Ans _____ m/hour

**44** A boat can travel 15km in 20 min. At the same rate how long will it take the boat to cover 75km?

Ans _____ hr _____ min

**45** What would you use to measure the length of a school desk? Circle one answer.

Thermometer     Trundle Wheel

Metre stick     Protractor     Litre jug

**46** Circle the best unit for measuring a large school playground. Circle one answer.

Millimetres          Metres

Centimetres          Kilometres

**47** A bank will exchange £1 for 7·92 French Francs. A hotel will exchange £1 for 7·50 French Francs. How much more will I get if I exchange £30 in the bank rather than in the hotel?

Ans _____ F.Francs

**48** 500 Spanish pesetas can be exchanged for £2 sterling. How many Spanish pesetas are worth £17 sterling?

Ans _____ Pesetas

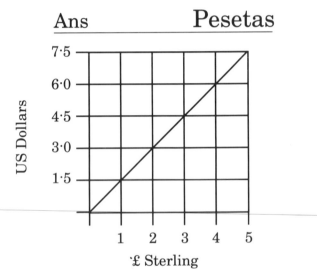

Look at this graph showing exchange rates between £ sterling and US dollars and answer the questions.

**49** How many US dollars are worth £3·50.

Ans _____ US $

**50** How many £ sterling are worth 6·75 US dollars.

Ans £ _____

# NUMBER 1

**1** Circle the largest number.

170    701    810    102    137    96

**2** Write six thousand and eight in figures.

Ans _____

**3** How many hundreds are in 6500?

Ans _____

**4** Circle the 5 which is worth 5 hundreds.

## 5   5   5   5

**5** One book costs £1.17. How much for 10?

Ans £ _____

**6** Multiply 245 by 100.

Ans _____

**7** Write the following as a decimal fraction.

$$\frac{3}{100} =$$ _____

**8** How many degrees centigrade between

## -7°C and +12°C?

Ans _____ °C

**9** How many degrees below zero is -34°C?

Ans _____ °C

**10** What is 8% of 100?

Ans _____

**11** What percentage of 100 is 15?

Ans _____ %

**12** How many eggs are in 9 boxes if each box holds 6 eggs?

Ans _____ eggs

**13** How many full boxes of sweets, holding 8 sweets each, could be filled using 64 sweets?

Ans _____ boxes

**14** How much is 75 less than 98?

Ans _____

**15** I had 37 toys and bought 17 more. How many toy cars do I have now?

Ans _____

**16** Calculate

$$\begin{array}{r} 78 \\ \times\, 9 \\ \hline \end{array}$$

**17** Calculate

$$8\overline{)93}$$
Rem

**18** From a 4 metre length of wood I cut 1.63 metres and then 2.08 metres. What length of wood is left?

Ans _____ m

**19** How much change do I have from £10.00 if I spend £3.90 and £4.25?

Ans £ _____

**20** How many 12p oranges can be bought using £1?

Ans _____ oranges

**21** A teacher takes a group of nine 8-year-old pupils to the seaside by train. The return fare is £2.30 per child and £4.80 per adult. How much in total does the teacher pay in return fares?

Ans £ _____

**22** 19 x 19 is approximately how many? Circle one answer.

40          140          400          440          4000

**23** 1287 − 195 is approximately how many? Circle one answer.

900          1000          1100          1150          1500

**24** This calculator display shows the average weight in grams of plums in a box. What is the weight to the nearest gram?

$$27.352$$

Ans _____ grams

**25** This calculator display shows the average wage earned by 8 workmen. What is their average wage to the nearest pound?

$$127.765$$

Ans £ _____

**26** Write 8 X 8 in index form.

Ans _____

**27** Calculate $5^3$.

Ans _____

**28** What fraction is equivalent to $\frac{1}{3}$? Circle one answer.

$\frac{3}{4}$          $\frac{2}{3}$          $\frac{2}{6}$          $\frac{1}{7}$          $\frac{1}{30}$

**29** What fraction is equivalent to $\frac{4}{10}$? Circle one answer.

$\frac{4}{5}$          $\frac{3}{5}$          $\frac{1}{7}$          $\frac{2}{5}$          $\frac{1}{10}$

**30** What fraction is the same as 75%? Circle one answer.

$\frac{7}{10}$          $\frac{3}{4}$          $\frac{75}{75}$          $\frac{1}{8}$          $\frac{1}{2}$

**31** What percentage is the same as $\frac{1}{5}$? Circle one answer.

10%          50%          75%          25%          20%

**32** 1 litre is approximately $1\frac{3}{4}$ pints. How many pints in 2 litres?

Ans _____ pints

**33** 1 inch is approximately $2\frac{1}{2}$ centimetres. How many centimetres in 6 inches?

Ans _____ cm

**34** Calculate

$$\begin{array}{r} 358 \\ \times\ 73 \\ \hline \end{array}$$

**35** Calculate

$$8\overline{)416}$$

**36** A coat originally costing £125 is sold at a discount of 10%. What does the coat cost now?

Ans £ _____

**37** In a box of 175 apples $\frac{2}{5}$ are rotten. How many apples are good?

Ans _____ apples

**38** By how many degress centigrade does the temperature drop in going from +19°C to -7°C?

Ans _____ °C

**39** A workman earned £200 per week and received a pay rise of 17%. How much does he earn per week now?

Ans £ _____

**40** Rental on a family home cost £240 per month. It is then increased by 5%. What is the monthly rent now?

Ans £ _____

**41** A square has an area of 66cm². Each side of the square has a length between which of the following? Circle one answer.

5cms & 6cm          8cm & 9cm

1cm & 2cm          3cm & 4cm

**42** A square with each side of length 9.6 cm has an area between which of the following? Circle one answer.

16cm² & 25cm²          36cm² & 49cm²

49cm² & 64cm²          81cm² & 100cm²

**43** A map is drawn to a scale of 5cm equals 12km. How many kilometres is 15cm equal to?

Ans _____ km

**44** 0.70 is equivalent to how many percent? Circle one answer.

7%          70%          75%          17%          77%

**45** A car cost £8000 but is increased in price by 8%. What is the new cost of the car?

Ans £ _____

**46** A bicycle is decreased in cost from £200 to £150. What is the percentage decrease in cost?

Ans _____ %

**47** In a school 30 children eat 3 bags of potatoes per week. At this same rate how many bags of potatoes would 90 children eat in 4 weeks?

Ans _____ bags

**48** A family's monthly income was £1200. The total monthly bills were £500. The income increased by 10% while the bills increased by 7%. After these percentage increases how much money is left after paying the bills?

Ans £ _____

**49** Round these numbers to the nearest 100 or nearest 10 and multiply them.

796 x 38

Ans _____

**50** Round these numbers to the nearest 100 or nearest 10 and divide them.

598 ÷ 22

Ans _____

---

## TEST TWO

---

**1** Write in words 12,009.

Ans _____

**2** Write in figures sixteen thousand, five hundred and twenty seven.

Ans _____

**3** What is the biggest number you can make with the figures 2, 4, 1 and 8?

Ans _____

**4** What is the value of the underlined figure?

3 <u>9</u> 5 6 4    Ans _____

**5** Which figure (digit) has the greatest value in this number? Circle one figure.

2 , 6 9 8

**6** Write the number shown the abacus.

Ans _____

**7** What number is 10 times greater than 57?

Ans _____

**8** 316 x _____ = 31600

**9** Write 3 metres and 97 centimetres as a decimal.

Ans _____ m

**10** Write 2 metres and 3 centimetres as a decimal.

Ans _____ m

**11** How many degrees between -7°C and +4°C?

Ans _____ °C

**12** What is 11% of 100?

Ans _____

**13** 42 toys out of 100 is how many percent?

Ans _____ %

**14** 7 x 8 =

**15** 63 ÷ ( ) = 9

**16** I have £27 more than John who has £38. How much have I?

Ans £ _____

**17** A jigsaw of 96 pieces has 18 pieces missing. How many pieces are there?

Ans _____ pieces

**18** A bus stopped to pick up 7, 6, 5, 6 and 3 passengers. How many passengers did it pick up?

Ans _____ passengers

**19** How much less than 758 is 467?

Ans _____

**20** How many eggs in 8 boxes if each box has 49 eggs?

Ans _____ eggs

**21** How much is left of a 3.5metre copper pipe if a man cuts from it a pipe 1.65 metres in length?

Ans _____ m

**22** What is the total weight of two parcels which weigh 3.6kg and 2.9kg?

Ans _____ kg

**23** A book has 162 pages. If I read 6 pages each day, how long will it take me to finish the book?

Ans _____ days

**24** If I save £1.25 each week from my pocket money, how much will I have after 8 weeks?

Ans £ _____

**25** Write this calculator display to the nearest whole number.

$$90 \cdot 07$$

Ans _____

**26** Calculate

$$2^2 + 5^2 + 3^2 = \text{Ans}$$

**27** What number 81 using index form.

Ans _____

**28** Complete the equation by putting the correct number in the box.

$$\frac{1}{2} = \frac{\Box}{10}$$

**29** Complete the equation by putting the correct number in the box.

$$\frac{\Box}{5} = \frac{40}{100}$$

**30** How many percent is equivalent to $\frac{1}{2}$?

Ans _____ %

**31** Which simple fraction is equivalent to 90%? Circle one answer.

$$\frac{1}{9} \qquad \frac{9}{10} \qquad \frac{9}{9} \qquad \frac{90}{90} \qquad \frac{19}{90}$$

**32** Write 37 in Roman numerals.

Ans _____

**33** Calculate

$$\begin{array}{r} 756 \\ \times\ 87 \\ \hline \end{array}$$

**34** Calculate

$$6\,|\,339$$

Rem

**35** In a train carrying 136 passengers $\frac{1}{4}$ of them were women and the rest men. How many men were on the train?

Ans _____ men

**36** What is $\frac{1}{5}$ of 2 kg?

Ans _____ kg

**37** A frozen cake costing £1.80 is increased in cost by 10%. How much does the cake rise in price?

Ans £ _____

**38** $\frac{1}{4}$ kg of very expensive sweets costs £5.00. How much do they cost per gram?

Ans £ _____

**39** A bank deposit account attracts 5% simple interest per year. I had £600 in my account for one year and then I added on my year's interest. How much is in my account now?

Ans £ _____

**40** What is the area of a square when each side measures 8 metres?

Ans _____ m²

**41** Paving slabs are £3 each and measure 1m X 1m square. How much would it cost me to cover a space measuring 3m X 7m using these slabs?

Ans £ _____

NUMBER 1 TEST TWO PAGE 3

**42** Circle the smallest number.

$$0.029 \quad 0.111 \quad 0.007$$
$$0.321 \quad 0.123$$

**43** Put these decimal fractions in ascending order (smallest first).

$$1.019 \quad 1.910 \quad 1.091$$
$$1.901 \quad 1.109$$

Ans _____

_____

**44** Circle the 2 which is worth 2 hundredths.

$$2 \ 2 \ 2 \ \cdot \ 2 \ 2 \ 2$$

**45** 0.4 is equivalent to how many percent? Circle one answer.

$$4\% \quad\quad 14\% \quad\quad 40\%$$
$$400\% \quad\quad 44\%$$

**46** A garden swing originally costing £125 is sold at a discount of 10%. How much is this less than the original cost?

Ans £ _____

**47** A racing car set originally costing £133 has its price increased by $\frac{1}{7}$ What is its new price?

Ans £ _____

**48** To paint a wall of 6 square metres requires $\frac{1}{2}$ litre of paint. Using paint at the same rate how much paint would I need to paint a wall measuring 36 square metres?

Ans _____ litres

**49** A family is planning to go to France on a camping holiday. The tour company quote a price of £850 but later write to the family saying there has been a 15% increase in the cost. What is the new price of the holiday?

Ans £ _____

**50** A bank offers to exchange £1 for 1.50 US dollars. How many US dollars ($) do you receive for £97?

Ans $ _____

# SHAPE AND SPACE

The lines in this shape are named by using capital letters. The base line is FC.

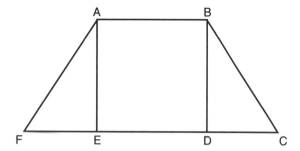

Which lines are perpendicular to FC?

**1** _____     **2** _____

**3** Name the line which is parallel to FC.

Ans _____

Name two oblique lines.

**4** _____     **5** _____

**6** The shape formed by ABDE is a

Ans _____

**7** How many horizontal lines are there?

Ans _____

**8** How many right angles are there?

Ans _____

Name these shapes. Complete the table by placing the letter of the shape beside its name.

A          B          C

D          E          F

| | |
|---|---|
| SQUARE | D |
| **9** KITE | _____ |
| **10** RECTANGLE | _____ |
| **11** TRAPEZIUM | _____ |
| **12** RHOMBUS | _____ |
| **13** PARALLELOGRAM | _____ |

Answer these questions about the shapes drawn above.

**14** Which shape has equal sides but not equal angles?

Ans _____

**15** How many of the shapes have 2 sets of parallel lines?

Ans _____

**16** Which shape has 2 pairs of equal sides which are not opposite to each other?

Ans _____

**17** Which shape does not have a line of symmetry?

Ans _____

**18** Which shape has only one pair of parallel sides?

Ans _____

Show all the lines of symmetry in each of these shapes.

**19**

**20**

**21**

**22**

By rotation find the order of rotational symmetry for each of these shapes.

**23**

rotational
symmetry of
order

Ans _____

**24**

rotational
symmetry of
order

Ans _____

**25**

rotational
symmetry of
order

Ans _____

**26**

rotational
symmetry of
order

Ans _____

In which direction would you be facing if you:

**27** Faced East and then turned clockwise through 2 right angles?

Ans _____

**28** Faced SW and turned anti-clockwise through $1\frac{1}{2}$ right angles?

Ans _____

**29** Faced West and turned 270° anticlockwise?

Ans _____

**30** Faced NE and turned 180° clockwise?

Ans _____

How many degrees from-

**31** North, clockwise to East?

Ans _____ °

**32** West, clockwise to South?

Ans _____ °

**33** SW, anticlockwise to NW?

Ans _____ °

**34** East, anticlockwise to NW?

Ans _____ °

Complete the table below by matching the shapes and nets.

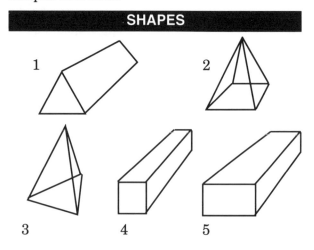

**SHAPES**

1  2  3  4  5

**NETS**

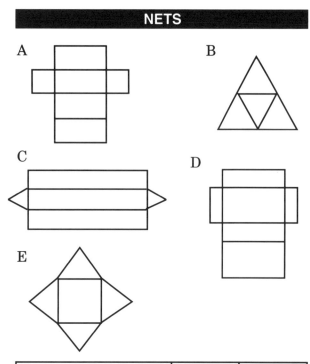

A  B  C  D  E

|  | Shape | Net |
|---|---|---|
| **35** Square pyramid |  |  |
| **36** Triangular pyramid |  |  |
| **37** Square prism |  |  |
| **38** Rectangular prism |  |  |
| **39** Triangular prism |  |  |

**40** How many faces has a rectangular prism?

Ans _____ faces

**41** How many faces has a triangular pyramid?

Ans _____ faces

**42** How many rectangular faces has a square prism?

Ans _____ faces

**43** How many square faces has a square prism?

Ans _____ faces

**44** How many vertices (corners) has a square pyramid?

Ans _____ vertices

**45** Which shape has 6 vertices?

Ans _____

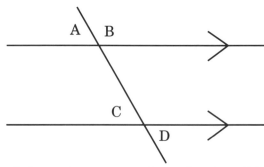

Read these statements about the size of the angles in the above diagram. Decide whether each statement is true or false. Write True or False for your answers.

**46** A is equal to C        Ans _____

**47** C is not equal to D        Ans _____

**48** B is equal to C        Ans _____

**49** B and D together make 180° Ans _____

**50** A and C together make 180° Ans _____

**1** Circle the hexagon.

**2** How many faces has a cuboid? Ans _____

**3** How many faces has a tetrahedron (triangular pyramid)?

Ans _____ faces

**4** How many vertices has a triangular prism?

Ans _____ vertices

**5** Circle the right-angled corner in this triangle.

**6** Calculate the angle at X.

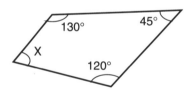

Ans _____ °

Complete these diagrams of shapes which are reflected in a mirror.

**7**

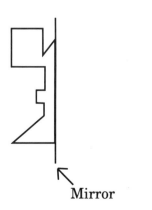

Mirror

**8**

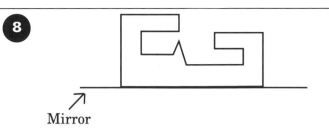

Mirror

**9**

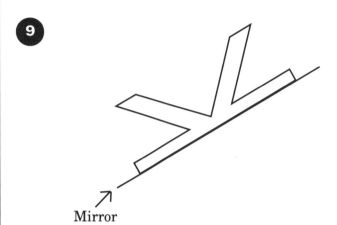

Mirror

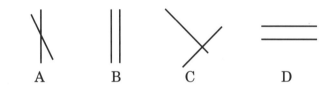

A     B     C     D

**10** Which of the above lines are perpendicular?   Ans _____

**11** Which of the above lines are horizontal?   Ans _____

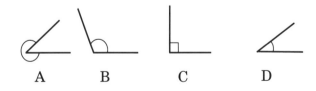

A     B     C     D

**12** Which angle is acute?   Ans _____

**13** Which angle is reflex?   Ans _____

Complete this table.

| | Name of solid | Number of Faces | Number of edges |
|---|---|---|---|
| **14** | Cube | 6 | |
| **15** | Triangular prism | | 9 |
| **16** **17** | Square based pyramid | | |

**18** What direction is directly opposite NE?

Ans _____

**19** How many degrees between E and NW going clockwise?

Ans _____ °

**20** If I turn 135° anticlockwise from NE in which direction do I face?

Ans _____

**21** I'm facing NW. If I turn 270° clockwise in which direction am I now facing?

Ans _____

Learning Together Island

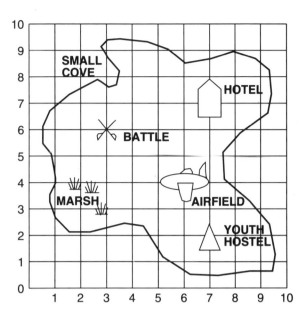

Look at the map of Learning Together Island.

**22** What can I find at (3,8)?

Ans _____

**23** What can I find at (6,4)?

Ans _____

**24** What are the co-ordinates of the youth hostel?

Ans ( ___ , ___ )

**25** What are the co-ordinates of the hotel?

Ans ( ___ , ___ )

**26** How many lines of symmetry has this shape?

Ans _____

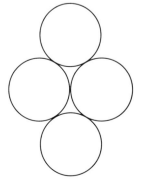

**27** Draw a line of symmetry on this shape.

**28** Draw a line of symmetry on this shape.

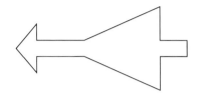

**29** How many degrees are at X?

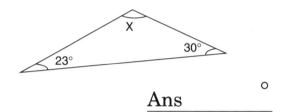

Ans _____ °

**30** How many degrees are at X?

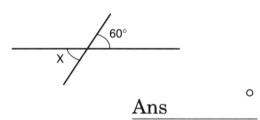

Ans _____ °

**31** How many degrees are at X?

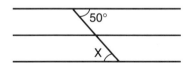

Ans _____ °

**32** Look at the shape on the left. Which shape on the right has been rotated by 180°? Circle one letter.

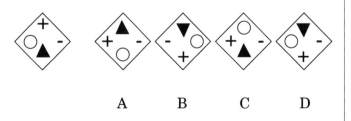

     A       B       C       D

**33** Look at the shape on the left. Which shape on the right has been rotated 90° anticlockwise? Circle one letter.

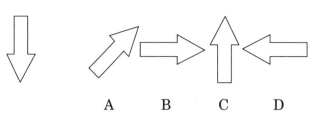

     A       B       C       D

**34** Look at the shape on the left. Which shape on the right has been rotated 90° anticlockwise? Circle one letter.

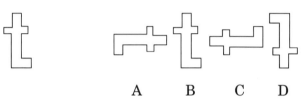

     A       B       C       D

**35** How many lines of symmetry has an equilateral triangle?

Ans _____

**36** Draw a line of symmetry on this oval shape.

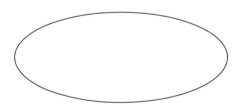

**37** Draw all the lines of symmetry on this Rhombus.

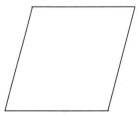

SHAPE AND SPACE TEST TWO PAGE 3

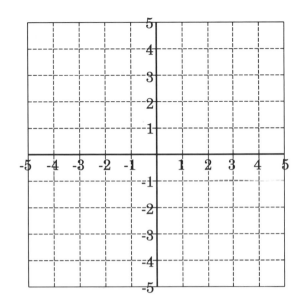

Mark these points on the above grid and label them.

**38** A (3, -2)

**39** B (-1, -2)

**40** C (-1, 2)

**41** D (3,2)

Circle the answer that completes this statement correctly.
Shapes that tessellate. . .

**42** a) are big.

b) join together without leaving spaces.

c) are round.

d) are always regular shapes.

**43** How many lines of symmetry has a regular pentagon?

Ans _____

**44** Draw all the lines of symmetry on this regular pentagon.

**45** This 2-D drawing represents a 3-D shape. What is the 3-D shape called?

Ans _____

**46** What shape will be formed by folding this net?

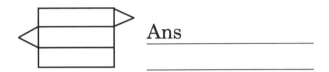

Ans _____

_____

**47** Look at this plan. Mark the most likely place for the front door using an X.

| CLOAK ROOM | KITCHEN |
|------------|---------|
| HALLWAY    |         |
| LIVING ROOM | DINING ROOM |

**48** Which of the following shapes is not drawn below? Circle one letter.

    A     RHOMBUS

    B     PARALLELOGRAM

    C     KITE

    D     TRAPEZIUM

**49** A square has an area of 49cm². Each side of the square is 7cm long. If each side is doubled in length how many times would the area increase?

Ans _____ times

**50** A square has sides each measuring 2cm. The length of each side is reduced to 1 cm. What fraction of the old area is the new area?

Ans _____

# NUMBER 2

SCORE:  TEST ONE _____

TEST TWO _____

Output numbers are produced from input numbers by using a certain rule. Work out the rule each time and enter the correct number in the box. A different rule is used for each question.

**1** Input → Output

2 → 7

5 → 10

10 → 15

14 → ☐

**2** Input → Output

1 → 5

4 → 20

7 → 35

10 → ☐

**3** Input → Output

3 → 1

15 → 5

21 → 7

30 → ☐

**4** Input → Output

5 → 11

8 → 17

10 → 21

12 → ☐

Supply the missing numbers.

**5** 12 + 14 = 20 + 2 + ☐

**6** 18 + 19 = 20 + ☐ + 9

**7** 27 + 25 = 40 + ☐ + 5

**8** 56 + 33 = 80 + 6 + ☐

**9** What are the three factors of 9?

☐ ☐ ☐

**10** What are the four factors of 15?

☐ ☐ ☐ ☐

**11** 12 has six factors. Enter them in the boxes.

☐ ☐ ☐ ☐ ☐ ☐

In each line below circle **2** numbers which are factors of 24.

**12** 4    5    10    12    16

**13** 2    7    8    14    20

**14** 1    9    18    20    24

Supply the missing multiples in each line.

**15** 0    4    8    12    16    ☐    ☐

**16** 0    10    20    ☐    40    ☐    60

**17** 0    7    ☐    21    28    ☐    42

**18** 0    ☐    18    27    ☐    45    54

Put the correct numbers in the boxes.

**19** 5 x 16 = 10 x ☐

**20** 2 x 12 = 4 x ☐

**21** 1 x 18 = 2 x ☐

**22** 50 x 40 = 100 x ☐

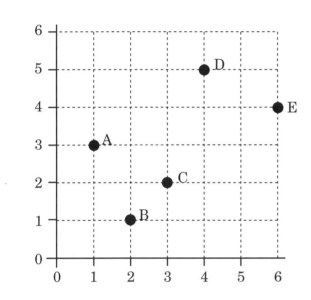

The letter A is at (1, 3). Give the co-ordinates for the following.

**23** Letter B ( _____ , _____ )

**24** Letter C ( _____ , _____ )

**25** Letter D ( _____ , _____ )

**26** Letter E ( _____ , _____ )

If 25 x 6 = 150

**27** then 150 ÷ ☐ = 25

**28** and 25 = ☐ ÷ 6

If 306 ÷ 18 = 17

**29** then 306 ÷ 17 = ☐

**30** and 17 x 18 = ☐

**31** $2^2$ = ☐     **32** $6^2$ = ☐

**33** $6^2 - 2^2$ = ☐

**34** $6^2 + 2^2$ = ☐

**35** $6^2 ÷ 2^2$ = ☐

**36** $\sqrt{64}$ = ☐

**37** $\sqrt{81}$ = ☐

**38** $\sqrt{121}$ = ☐

Circle the prime number in each line.

**39**   4       6       8       9       13       16

**40**   20     21     24     25     27     29

**41**   40     42     43     45     46     49

---

**42** Multiply 9 by 7 and take-away 4. ☐

**43** Divide 15 by 3 and multiply by 8. ☐

**44** Take 25 from 74 and divide by 7. ☐

---

**45** $35 \div x = 7$
What is the value of x? ☐

**46** $y - 14 = 31$
What is the value of y? ☐

**47** $3z - 14 = 10$
What is the value of z? ☐

---

$a = 3$   $b = 7$   $c = 8$
Calculate the following.

**48** $a(b+c) =$ ☐

**49** $ab+c =$ ☐

**50** $b(c-a) =$ ☐

Output numbers are produced from input numbers by using a certain rule. Work out the rule each time and enter the correct number in the box. A different rule is used for each question.

Put the correct numbers in the squares.

**1** Input → Output

| 4 | → | 10 |
| 8 | → | 14 |
| 10 | → | 16 |
| 19 | → | ☐ |

**2** Input → Output

| 3 | → | 8 |
| 5 | → | 12 |
| 10 | → | 22 |
| 14 | → | ☐ |

**3** Input → Output

| 2 | → | 12 |
| 5 | → | 30 |
| 8 | → | 48 |
| 10 | → | ☐ |

**4** Input → Output

| 32 | → | 7 |
| 28 | → | 6 |
| 20 | → | 4 |
| 8 | → | ☐ |

If 26 x 6 = 156

**5** then 26 = 156 ÷ ☐

**6** and 26 x 60 = ☐

If 27 x 13 = 351

**7** then 351 ÷ 27 = ☐

**8** and ☐ x 13 = 3510

**9** 5 x ☐ = 10 x 12

**10** 17 x 4 = 34 x ☐

**11** 8 x 36 = ☐ x 18

---

**12** Which multiples of 3 are greater than 1 but less than 10?

Ans

**13** Which multiples of 8 are greater than 40 but less than 70?

Ans

**14** List the common multiples of 2 and 5 which are less than 40 but greater than 1.

Ans

**15** List the common multiples of 4 and 6 which are less than 40 but greater than 20.

Ans

Complete the multiplication table.

**16**

| X | 7 | |
|---|---|---|
| 3 | | |
| 8 | | 40 |
| | 42 | |

**17** **18**

**19**

**20** **21**

List the common factors of each pair of numbers.

**22** 4 and 10    Ans _____

**23** 8 and 36    Ans _____

**24** 6 and 12    Ans _____

Give the highest common factor of each pair.

**25** 9 and 12    ☐

**26** 10 and 45   ☐

**27** 18 and 36   ☐

**28** Which factors of 15 are prime numbers?

Ans _____

**29** List the prime numbers which are greater than 10 but less than 20.

Ans _____

**30** Five numbers, less than 20, are triangular numbers. List them.

| 1 | 3 | | | |
|---|---|---|---|---|

**31** Take 9 away from 17 and multiply the answer by 9.

Ans _____

**32** Multiply 8 by 6 and divide by 12.

Ans _____

**33** Divide 100 by 5 and take away 7.

Ans _____

**34** Multiply 5 by 7 and add on three times 6.

Ans _____

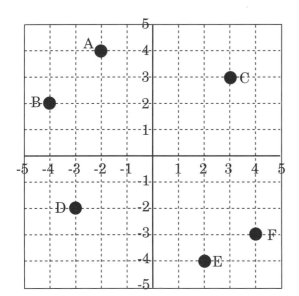

The letter A is at (-2, 4) and F is at (4, -3)

Give the co-ordinates of

**35** B ( _____ , _____ )

**36** C ( _____ , _____ )

**37** D ( _____ , _____ )

**38** E ( _____ , _____ )

_____

**39** $10^2 - 5^2 =$ ☐

**40** $9^2 + 1^2 =$ ☐

**41** $2^2 \times 3^2 =$ ☐

**42** $1^3 = 1 \times 1 \times 1 =$ ☐

**43** $2^3 = 2 \times 2 \times 2 =$ ☐

**44** $3^3 =$ ☐

**45** $4^3 =$ ☐

**46** $3^3 - 2^3 =$ ☐

**47** $4^3 \times 1^3 =$ ☐

_____

x = 4          y = 6          z = 9

Calculate the following.

**48** $xy + yz =$ ☐

**49** $x (z - y) =$ ☐

**50** $(x + y) (y + z) =$ ☐